LifeStyle
NetWorthing

Integrating Personal & Professional Relationships

Emmy ~
Be blessed as you celebrate
the blessings of others!
Polly   3-30-14

Polly Rhea Harper

For requests, contact: Polly Rhea Harper, polly@pollyharper.com, 1-678-562-0290

Printed in the United States of America

978-0-9914695-0-5

1. Sales 2. Business 3. Self-Help Techniques 4. Spirituality

Project Management – Bonnie Daneker at Write Advisors, Atlanta, GA
Cover design - Sophie Gibson at Vivo360, Inc., Alpharetta, GA
Book design - Debbie Kerr at Plan Bee, Tucker, GA

Foreword

*A*s I climbed into bed after midnight, I was so anxious to read this book that I spent the next hour consumed with the message. I read slowly, trying to take in each word. What comes through clearly in the stories is the core of "NetWorthing." Prior to reading this book, I accepted the term "NetWorthing" as "Polly being Polly" but wasn't sure anyone else could ever be the same or believe they could approach business in the same manner.

I thought a book on "NetWorthing" was surely not for everyone, but was just going to be a self-portrait of an amazing lady with an amazing concept to networking. Instead, I found it to be an approach that everyone could use, will feel they should use at some level, and will be inspired to try (even in small ways at first). By keeping the word "NetWorthing" prominent in the book, it presents a single clear theme versus a book of random concepts.

The quotes introduce faith without pushing religion into a reader's face, instead causing them to consider a very important approach to business and life.

All who read this will look at relationships in a new light – the NetWorthing way.

Loren Burke
Retired Technology Executive

Acknowledgements

A career and new lifestyle began for me in Atlanta, Georgia with a chain of divine events as Bill Leonard, President and Founder of Wm. Leonard & Co. trusted God about a stranger from Texas with few known references.

Bill is truly an entrepreneur with extraordinary vision. His faith in God and the freedom he gave me to operate within my strengths allowed us to participate in new horizons for Wm. Leonard & Co. It was God who rewarded and blessed our efforts.

This journey has become a LifeStyle of NetWorthing in business. It developed naturally over time through many different opportunities. It was made possible only through the atmosphere of encouragement that Bill allowed to happen. As a result, NetWorthing flourished. Our basic belief is to choose people as our first priority and trust God to provide the business.

God has rewarded me personally and professionally in many ways. I certainly give most of the credit to Bill Leonard, whose insight and vision God used to create the path that I followed.

Generosity should always be recognized with praise in my opinion. I never discuss this writing project without mentioning Bonnie Daneker, CEO of Write Advisors. This book would not exist without her spirit of generosity and expertise. She quickly captured the essence of my message and gently guided me through the process. Bonnie has a servant's heart, always respecting the Author. *NetWorthing with Polly - Meet Bonnie at www.WriteAdvisors.com*

More than once, my friend Sophie Gibson, President of Vivo360, Inc., freely demonstrated her friendship. She puts words into action as she expresses her friendship. As if running a successful digital marketing company was not enough, she still takes time to help friends. It may be her beautiful cover design that invited you to visit the inside of this book. *NetWorthing with Polly - Meet Sophie at www.vivo360inc.com*

The accurate and tactful delivery of an editor must be tough when assisting a first-time author. Cherie Peters, Founder of Mary's Catholic Garden Book Store and editor of this book, showed herself capable of delivering words correctly without removing my voice from the message. *NetWorthing with Polly – Meet Cherie at www.MarysCatholicGarden.com*

Debbie Kerr of Plan Bee created the artistic design for the interior pages of the book. Her work helped move it from a manuscript to the desirable and enjoyable format that you now hold in your hands. *NetWorthing with Polly – Meet Debbie at www.PlanBee.biz*

BookLogix created a means for the book to be self-published and reach people outside my sphere of influence. Our goal was to make it easily available to the public and they have done that for a new audience.

I do very little without friends. Listed below are a few of "Those Who 'Brung' Me" to this place in life. They deserve to share in the book.

Georgia Herod, my friend of 46 years and retired English professor, in Missouri pointed out expressions used that were not saying what she knew I really wanted to say and challenged me to rethink and rewrite the words. James Shinn directed me to the best title choice. Peggy Cox in Texas believed in me and kept telling me to continue. Karen Mae Sledge offered marketing assistance. Cindra Vaden, a partner in almost all my projects, is always available for administrative advice.

With special affection, I thank the "Friends of Polly" (FOP) who have shared year after year in the Annual Ladies' Brunch. Your warm and loving spirits have touched many lives, including mine. Rich Cohen and Pat Poersch, our volunteer valet attendants each year, are our men in shining armor.

Many others, perhaps more than required, have proofread earlier versions of the book without sabotaging my efforts. Thanks to all of you who have helped and encouraged me along the way. Please take credit and share in any future success.

Dave Mims was heaven sent as my friend and has been a faithful inspiration in my Christian walk. God continues to teach me more about unconditional love through Dave. His endorsement makes me proud!

Suzie Price is a friend and an accomplished author. She inspired me to consider the work as a "calling." What an honor to have her words of professional wisdom as an endorsement. I am blessed indeed.

Without question, God had a plan for this book from the very beginning. I continue to be amazed at the unveiling of His master plan. He began something beyond my expectations and will complete it in all of us.

Contents

Introduction

"I make friends for a living."

When people asked about my career, that was my response (more often than not). After a while, it began to sound like a strange comment. For you see, it is my business to seek and establish new client relationships.

As pure as my motives were, that remark raised a negative connotation that I had to rethink. I sat down one night and began to put my thoughts on paper. Amazingly, that led to the beginning of this book.

As much as my heart and philosophy were in tune to building relationships, I had to reevaluate my behavior. Was there something I needed to do to balance my behavior to secure new business? The relationship factor was second nature to me, but it was not the complete business model. Relationships have to be kept pure but career goals need to be met. In other words, we need to allow relationships to be our main priority and let finances be an overflow of success. We should strive to maintain a healthy perspective between financial success and successful relationships.

The buzzword in our business culture today is "networking." It encourages us to get out, meet people and grow business. Although I agree that this is true, "NetWorthing" is the silver lining to networking. NetWorthing is where the exchange of divine encounters takes place, creating good value and relationships. The Bible undisputedly teaches that what we do in life returns to either bless us or curse us. Therefore, the investment we make in the life of another person should always be a blessing. Very few of us would refuse that return on investment.

"NetWorthing," a concept and practice, has been around since Jesus spoke profound words that have lingered through time.

> *Do to others whatever*
> *you would like them to do to you ...*
> *Matthew 7:12 NLT*

Back in the New Testament days, the most influential men of the time were called by Jesus to change their priorities and invest in others. If this was important then, it certainly should be important today. Some principles are simply timeless.

As I built my career with Wm. Leonard & Co. in commercial real estate, I made it my business to get to know everyone I could in the community. I tried to discover ways to enrich others. Often I found that it was through a real estate need, but more often, it was through a job search, a faith connection, a friendly introduction to someone or simply a warm hug or smile. As I strive to serve others, my life has become abundantly blessed.

Join me on the journey as we evaluate relationship priorities through the prism of NetWorthing. As we explore together, perhaps we can find that balance between our relationships and our business practices.

There are "friends" who destroy each other,
but a real friend sticks closer than a brother.

Proverbs 18:24 NLT

1
Worth a Million

1
Worth a Million

Several years ago, I made a call that I will never forget. For a long time I had heard about a particular software company, but had never met its president. One day I was inspired to call and tell him that I would really like to get to know the person behind the name. He typically did not take cold calls, but this was one of those exceptional times. He later said he was shocked that he had accepted my call, and was even more shocked when he agreed to meet for lunch. I knew right away that he was "worth a million" on my relationship meter. This was definitely a relationship worth keeping. I don't think I even discussed his real estate needs that day though I was able to help him later with those. Instead, we took some time to get to know one another finding we had many mutual friends and shared a common faith. This man and his entire family have become extended family to me. They are friends, family and clients, in that order. What a blessing they have become!

We can trust this familiar saying: "People are worth more than fame and fortune." While assets of treasure and gold are side benefits, we need to remember that they are the lesser value and our focus should be on people.

When we treasure someone our heart follows also. Placing our heart's desire in another person is only the beginning of a fulfilling experience with them. I firmly believe that the greatest investment you can make is in the life of another person. Whenever you find a person you consider to be "worth a million," your own life becomes more transparent, enabling you to see clearly that you are the recipient of many blessings. With each decision and with each hour spent, we will have our reward when we take the time to focus on the people amidst the circumstances of our business dealings. Perhaps this principle is somewhat akin to creating fertile soil in which to plant our seeds of success. We cannot grow a plant and enjoy its benefits if we have not spent time tilling the soil. Preparation and maintenance are absolutely necessary for success. Some plants fade or wilt, but when the soil is properly cultivated, we can continue to reap results from what the soil produces later. The abundant life is in the soil we have diligently fertilized and watered.

> *Don't be misled – you cannot mock*
> *the justice of God.*
> *You will always harvest what you plant.*
> *Galatians 6:7 NLT*

The special person in our life that we call "one in a million" will bring us unlimited joy and sustenance as long as we deposit the proper nutrients of time and energy.

The next time we are seeking to increase sales or select a service, let's keep our eyes on the people involved in the business deal. We should look for integrity and character to establish a proper relationship. It will create a worthwhile foundation for this and future relationships. One thing is sure: when our focus is elsewhere, it will be obvious to everyone.

Our actions will not be accepted with the same grace and grit as when we treat each other with sincerity and sensitivity. Cash is not king but a "cash-out" from a journey in NetWorthing pays great dividends.

"The greatest investment we can make

is in the life of another person."

2
Worth a Thousand Words

2
Worth a Thousand Words

One day, I read an article in a tech magazine about the work ethic of an executive. Because I was touched by his discipline and management style, I spontaneously called him late that afternoon. I was delighted to have a short conversation, in which he mentioned his upcoming employee meeting. Eagerly the next morning, I rushed to pick up a dozen donuts to take to his office. As he passed the front desk for his meeting, I introduced myself for the first time and handed him the donuts for that meeting. I can still see the astonished look on his face as we shook hands and went our separate ways. It only seemed like moments since we had hung up the phone. Even I was amazed! He told me to stay in touch, which I did on occasion. I would contact him whenever I noticed articles about his company and would occasionally invite him to business events.

Little did I know at the time I brought donuts that he would soon have a need to relocate and ask us to represent him and his company. When my new friend had a real estate need, he advised his CFO to call our company to schedule an interview even though the CFO already had an existing real estate relationship. My friend made the decision to use the services of Wm. Leonard & Co. What an amazing endorsement and what a tremendous blessing to us! Our company helped with his company's relocation and further expansions as they grew.

Did I call this executive with an ulterior motive? Absolutely not! But did I receive two-fold from the random act of kindness? Absolutely yes! I gained a real estate client and a friend, as well as a memorable heartfelt return on my investment. The physical act of kindness spoke louder than any presentation I could have made. Perhaps my actions were "worth a thousand words!"

A truly wise person uses few words;
a person with understanding is even-tempered.
Even fools are thought wise when they keep silent;
with their mouths shut, they seem intelligent.

Proverbs 17:27, 28 NLT

NetWorthing experiences like this one provide me with an abundant lifestyle. Unfortunately, it doesn't happen every day, but I encourage everyone to try. Begin pouring yourselves into others to see the way God can be alive and real. How we "depict" ourselves is through our actions: we create a picture of us for others to see.

A picture is worth a thousand words. How many times in our lives have we heard that said? Probably more than we can count. How many times have we thought about our lives in terms of being a positive reflection to someone else, especially within the business world? Another buzzword used in the business community today is called "branding." Our strongest personal brand is the one portrayed to people we encounter on life's journey. It should be natural and authentic, serving others with acts of kindness.

Consider these questions when interacting with prospects and clients:

- How do they see our actions as we present business plans?
- Does the image we present tell them we recognize their need?
- Do they see that we have their best interests in mind?
- Do they see integrity or inferiority?
- Do they see truth or doubt?
- Do they see courage or corruption?
- Do they see transparency or a facade?

There is no need to "sell" if we have found a way to provide results and satisfy the buyer. That's good for both of us. However, if we are unable to fulfill their needs, then maybe we should honestly admit to them that this is not the best solution for them. Maybe we serve them best by walking away from the deal and by offering possible alternatives.

No one should be sold something he doesn't really want or need, right? We need to do the honorable thing.

When people look at you or me and say, "There goes an honorable person; I like doing business with him (or her)," we are branded as a success in their mind. It would be good for us to remember and treasure that picture of honorable success, as it will become a new and "living" brand for us. For indeed a picture is "worth a thousand words."

NetWorthing with Polly

$$\infty$$

"There goes an honorable person;

I like doing business with him (or her)."

3
Worth the Wait

3
Worth the Wait

Several years ago, I met the president of a local corporation after hearing him give a talk at church. You are right to think that it was not the typical setting for a talk on business. I didn't see potential business in it for me at the time nor did I perceive that our Annual High Tech Prayer Breakfast would one day be established and include him.

On Sunday, I heard this president speak about his faith, family and work. If nothing else, it filled my heart with a new encouragement. My professional energy was charged. As I reflected on my impressions, I thought, "He just has to meet the president of the company where I work. They have so much in common." With a sense of urgency, I initiated a potential meeting via letter between the two men so they could become acquainted. I explained my new instincts and reasons for the invitation. It did cross my mind that there was a long shot for a business deal, but it was not my main priority. The joy of a potential new relationship of this nature was reward enough for me at the time. Soon, the president's executive assistant graciously responded to the invitation to arrange an appointment for the luncheon. What a thrill! However something interfered with that meeting date, and the lunch never happened; the timing was not right. But the story continues!

One year later, our company became a sponsor of a community business event. As part of that sponsorship, we were encouraged to host a separate event during the month of October to celebrate technology. With an eager spirit, our president stopped by my office one morning and said, "I've got it; we will have a prayer breakfast for our special event!" Without so much as a second's pause, I replied, "And I know who we will have as our keynote speaker!" The rest of the story is history. The president who had spoken at church was invited as our keynote speaker and his speech was outstanding. The breakfast became an annual event and we invited him back six years later. There is no doubt in my mind that the day we met was a divine encounter leading to the breakfast. It was absolutely "worth the wait."

Sometimes you have to wait to do something right, like we waited a year to connect these two gentlemen. "Anything worth doing is worth doing right" is another way to reflect on this situation. Whether we are in pursuit of new relationships or something else, we should establish a reputation of excellence. It would be even better to have a reputation of trustworthiness. Trust is definitely considered a key component of our lives. When money is a part of the equation, excellence and trust are crucial. These virtues are key; when either is violated, our relationships suffer.

Because trust is so very important, the relationship should not be rushed. In many cases, the surest path to success for both is to be cautious, and to place a higher value on the person than the sale. There may be exceptions when the principle of supply and demand is a priority. Perhaps we have a unique need for a supplier and there are no other competitors. In that case, we are limited and must use the only available source. When there are no other options available, ethics in pricing becomes even more critical. From a sales perspective, we might be tempted to take an unfair advantage even though it is unethical.

> *Don't be selfish; don't try to impress others.*
> *Be humble, thinking of others as better than yourselves.*
> *Don't look out only for your own interests,*
> *but take an interest in others, too.*
>
> *Philippians 2:3, 4 NLT*

But in situations where the balance of trust is equal, both parties may be content to allow extra time for a deal to close, because we know we can rely on the other party. Ideal business alliances like this can still be stressful, but improving the atmosphere will demonstrate a much stronger commitment and loyalty.

Done right, a relationship will bring both parties mutual benefits. They will both know it was "worth the wait" to build the relationship based on trust and excellence!

NetWorthing with Polly

"*Anything worth doing is worth doing right!*"

4
Worth Repeating

4
Worth Repeating

*I*n business, we like to think that a job well done creates loyalty from our clients. We want them to invite us to repeat the service the next time there is a need. It does not always depend on our behavior; but many times, it does!

Imagine the picture of a small child after he has just experienced a special thrill with a friend. Can't you hear him as he excitingly repeats this statement, "Please do it again – do it again!" I think most of us can visualize it, or at least remember it happening at some time in our past.

Take that image and transfer it to a business setting. We don't usually scream out with excitement, but we do express our feelings in other ways. When someone does something right, we want them to do it again. When someone's performance exceeds our expectations, we notice, we reflect, and often we are inspired to act.

> *Iron sharpens iron,*
> *so one man sharpens another.*
> *Proverbs 27:17 NAS*

Consider venture capitalists for a moment. They are typically impressed with a new and exciting kind of technology, because they see future money. They invest, they labor and they promote the company for multiple returns. However, when it comes time for another project, do they hire new leadership? More than likely, they do not. The experience of the investment, due to the executive team, made their portfolio company a success. Said another way, they bet on the jockey, not the horse. Are we compelling agents that draw clients back to us for repeat business? I hope we are and that we can measure positive results.

Once again we recognize that true worth is found in the people, not the process. Let's identify our true worth, validate that worth and then accentuate those positive attributes. People notice. We develop a pathway to success that offers rich returns for us and for those around us. We identify and model a lifestyle of success. Many observe our model and adopt it for themselves. We should ask ourselves, "Are my actions and attitudes 'worth repeating'?"

NetWorthing with Polly

❦

"Please do it again – do it again!"

5
Worth the Effort

5
Worth the Effort

A s many days play out, we talk to strangers on the telephone while reaching out for new business. This was one of those times, and we became instant friends. We planned to meet for the first time at the upcoming meeting of the Southeastern Software Association. Once I entered the room, I saw a man in the distance looking toward me with a smile of verification. We seemed to know each other in a moment. We were both eager to exchange a warm hug and begin the constant conversation. That was our beginning. He was Founder and CEO of his own company, so it meant a possible future client for me. The friendship continued, and a real estate need did eventually develop.

A side story adds to the scenario. One of our clients sold his company about that time and was looking to get involved with another start-up company. Because both executives had faith in us as business professionals, they trusted the personal advice we offered. Before long, we introduced them to each other. The CEO friend was in need of an investment to take his company to the next phase. The other client was a CFO and was interested in investing in a new company. They soon became investment partners, resulting in a new real estate transaction. Guess who won that real estate assignment? We did. Fostering a relationship can have fruitful, long-term consequences.

These two businessmen were able to develop a long-lasting business relationship and friendship, which continued even after the sale of the company years later. I must say that the CEO is now one of my closest friends. Since our initial meeting, the CEO's wife and three children have become part of our relationship as well: It is with pleasure that I share my life with another adopted family. Deep and abiding friendships are a gift and even now, it would be hard to say which came first, the business or the friendship. It is a wonderful way to live – at work and at play – the line blurs if we aren't watching closely.

Always do a good job; be consistent and thoughtful in the treatment of clients and sales people, whatever position they hold. These lessons are simple but powerful. The consequences can go a very long way. "You cannot give out enough goodness," I like to say. Goodness is a virtue that follows us as we walk through life. Whether in business or not, it could be our most important and most valued companion.

Many people notice our diligence as much as our actual ability. We all want to become associated with winners and become winners ourselves. In that regard, we are noticed for what we accomplish, as well as the way we accomplish it. Some people are known to be rude and rough around the edges, but at the same time are respected for their tenacity. This is not a perfect model, but a model that works for some, some of the time. Does this describe us? If so, is this the kind of role model we want to be for other people in our lives?

Yet those who wait for the Lord will gain new strength;
they will mount up with wings like eagles. They will run and
not get tired. They will walk and not become weary.

Isaiah 40:31 NAS

Remember our thoughts from an earlier chapter on branding? Thinking of the role model scenario above, I am reminded of an advertisement where a man is sitting under a tree with his young son. Each time he makes a move, the son mirrors his action. Do we want each move we make to be significant and to be received with a positive attitude? If so, we need to be careful before we act.

Business environments create an opportunity for constant daily growth for each one of us. Therefore, it behooves us to pay attention to personal and professional habits, making sure that we are growing in virtue. This is our free continuing education!

As we look around is there someone that we can share time with under a tree? When we model good behavior and we can positively impact others, then we can acknowledge it was "worth the effort."

NetWorthing with Polly

"You cannot give out enough goodness!"

6
Worth Sharing

6
Worth Sharing

*T*here was a reason for our meeting. While I needed a residential real estate agent for the sale of my house, I didn't expect to find a life long friend as well. This new agent represented me beyond my expectations with excellence and professionalism during the sales transaction. We had a lot in common as single ladies, but I think that her attention to detail went above and beyond the call of duty. I was happy to refer her to others. As it turned out, I had need of her services again a few years later. She took care of the sale of my house after I relocated to a new one. When I later relocated out of town, she freely gave advice, but simply as a friend, commission free. We developed mutual respect and trust which made it a pleasure for me to refer her to others.

Do the right thing. When we work toward mutual trust, we will not be disappointed. Recommendations, good and bad, are shared. When we are known to be trustworthy, the word gets around. Once it is shared, it is usually shared again. In the future, others may speak to us as someone "worth sharing."

With each and every investment we make as we strengthen our business alliances, our referrals will gain momentum. People are well connected, and – whether we ask for a referral or not – when a relationship is established, a referral becomes automatic. (This includes the negative ones.) If our associations are of like character, our value is recognized and multiplies for our benefit.

A "good word" about people is not only shared through a formal recommendation letter, but can also be shared through body language. It can happen on the golf course, over lunch or at business events. We should never underestimate the power of the unspoken word. This kind of communication is valid and can sometimes go viral.

In these days of ever-so-popular social media, it has become the norm to ask for an online introduction by a trusted partner. We cannot keep our actions and attitudes hidden; they follow us everywhere we go.

Our digital footprint may be our demise: Once we hit "send" on the Internet, we cannot take it back.

We should be honest, sincere, credible and consistent in our effort to build rapport. This helps maintain the kind of personal brand that stimulates success.

Sometimes a remarkable outcome appears to take us by surprise. With this thought in mind, let's always remember that our reputation follows us. We cannot hide from it.

On the flip side of that scenario, we can sometimes leave the wrong impression and do more damage than good. Correcting a negative impression can be extremely difficult, but we should not live in fear. We should always remain true to our convictions and transparent in thought and deed. People recognize truth even in subtle ways.

Give, and it will be given to you.
They will pour into your lap a good measure —
pressed down, shaken together and running over.
For by your standard of measure it will be measured to you
in return.

Luke 6:38 NAS

NetWorthing with Polly

❧

"*We should never underestimate the*

power of the unspoken word!"

7
Worth Celebrating

7
Worth Celebrating

F riends are the greatest gift in life. Other than spiritual rewards, I do not know anything that brings more pleasure. I can say with pride that my richest treasures in life are due to those who allowed me into their lives as a trusted friend. All the riches in the world could not buy the treasure of friendships. Celebrate all of them! Recently a special group in Atlanta celebrated their 10th year of leadership and service awards to the community. They gathered nominations for many people who do exactly what is expressed in this book, but are typically not recognized for their actions. It was with joy that I was rewarded with a nomination. Even though I did not receive an award, I knew that those who won did so because of their unsung investment in other people. And, because of this wonderful event honoring them, I made new friendships with other nominees and award winners. What a fabulous tribute to those who make this event possible, and what a special way to be "celebrated." To celebrate with them and their awardees annually, visit www.turknett.com.

The message of this chapter is simple: Let's do good and celebrate others doing good. Before we can celebrate goodness, we must do something deemed significant. If we are truly experiencing meaningful relationships, we have much to celebrate and much for others to celebrate with us. It may be only one encounter with an individual or it may be repeated encounters with one or many individuals. Whatever the case may be, make it memorable in a positive way. A good comparison would be the concept of separating the chaff from the wheat. When the wheat is thrown up in the air the chaff blows away and the good part falls down. Speaking in terms of relationships, some people are receptive to our relationship investment and continue to be productive while others seem to depart without ever touching our souls.

When we look back on our experiences with others, do we find them to be inspirational? Are we always moving forward by investing in others? Do we celebrate life and meaningful relationships? If we are truly experiencing meaningful relationships, we have much to celebrate and much for others to celebrate with us. Who do we value as our most meaningful relationships? The most cherished and celebrated asset of all is our legacy, how people will feel about us after we are gone – Their reflection reminds us of a life worth living and a life worth remembering. We might even consider it our aroma of faith! Let not our hearts be troubled! If we have made our mark, so to speak, by treasuring others and being a treasure to them, then our lives count more than we know. We can be thankful and continue to make more investments. Be blessed as you celebrate the blessings of others! Let's create a life "worth celebrating!"

And may the Lord, the God of your
ancestors, multiply you a thousand times
more and bless you as He promised!
Deuteronomy 1:11 NLT

NetWorthing with Polly

"Be blessed as you celebrate

the blessings of others!"

8
Worth Ultimate Praise

8
Worth Ultimate Praise

I truly believe that the blessings I receive along the road of life are a result of God's unconditional love. The greatest of all credit is due to the Giver of eternal life. Because God in Heaven sent his Son to Earth to exchange His life for mine, I can have a life of victory and love.

In the previous chapter, we talked about meaningful relationships and celebration. Now I want to acknowledge my relationship with God, which surpasses all others. Years ago, I accepted His invitation to join Him on the greatest journey of NetWorthing. On this journey, He has shown me His unconditional love and often it is revealed through friends like you. That love is not unique just for me, but for all of us.

Faith in Jesus Christ is the beginning of what the Bible calls "abundant life" and is available to everyone exactly as He promised. All I needed to do was to ask forgiveness and believe in Him with my whole heart. I realize now that forgiveness was the key allowing His Spirit to live in and through me forever. That life has already begun. There is no need to wait for physical death to enter into an abundant life. However, I must die to my old nature through a life of obedience to allow the Holy Spirit to empower me.

This faith gives me the freedom to relate to people in a vibrant way and hide nothing about myself.

Divine opportunities are available to me through a biblically based real estate company and through High Tech Ministries (HTM), a 501 (c) (3) non-profit organization. It is in this environment that God allows me to openly and appropriately share with others both the faith and the hope that lives within me. For the first 10 years at HTM, I was point person to seek others with like faith to join the group as hosts for our annual High Tech Prayer Breakfast.

Growing together by sharing our hopes and challenges is an added benefit of personal relationships in business. Atlanta glows with light from people that I meet on a regular basis. Life is full of richness and lends us a measure of hope to live above the circumstances of this world. But when life does throw us challenges, we should always remember to learn from the experience and help others to learn also. We need to recognize those in trouble and offer to help them when we can.

> *For God has not given us a spirit of fear and timidity,*
> *but of power, love, and self-discipline.*
>
> 2 Timothy 1:7 NLT

Can you understand why I find it so joyful to meet new people every day? Can you understand why I am eager and willing to help others in need and sometimes put the business at hand as a second priority? I hope you can see why I am compelled to share insights into personal and professional relationships, and how I might long for you to share this same fulfillment.

Only God can confirm the hope and joy necessary to live a life of faith. He has a plan for each of us and wants us to walk in it with confidence. It is my prayer that we not only share a common professional philosophy, but that we are united in our faith journey also.

NetWorthing with Polly

"*Only God can confirm the*

hope and joy

necessary to live a life of faith."

9
Worthwhile Conclusion

9
Worthwhile Conclusion

*I*n the thoughts proposed, did we discover a good answer for the questions regarding a healthy balance between our personal and professional business relationships?

I believe the solution lies in the discipline we use, and the emphasis we choose. Even in our business environment, we need to remember to use things, not people. Often our motivation to reach career goals comes from those very people who inspire us personally. They motivate us to accomplish things in life but we must accomplish the work. To reach and maintain our goals in business, we must be diligent, deliberate and decisive. Always appreciate people and receive rewards in humility.

As in a poem, it is not really the words we read in black and white but rather the intention in the heart of the poet whose voice rings loud and clear. I hope you have read between the lines of these pages and heard the love in my heart, so that some of these things resonate in your heart.

Search me, O God, and know my heart;
test me and know my anxious thoughts.
Point out anything in me that offends you,
and lead me along the path of everlasting life.

Psalm 139:23-24 NLT

This little book is NOT meant to be only a momentary reflection. With multiple lessons on each page, it should be a "cheat sheet" for life to remind us to appreciate others and affirm our lives and theirs. Please embrace these thoughts carefully within your own philosophy and make them meaningful, relevant and realistic with your actions. They will be only fleeting thoughts otherwise.

A worthwhile conclusion is two-fold: 1) Relationships should always be value-based and full of dignity. They should flow in conjunction with business goals. 2) Be solid in all your business dealings. Successful businessmen and businesswomen have many common traits. At the top of the list, I place tenacity and good communication skills. Whether we offer a service or a product, we need to relay its competitive advantage and confirm that the other person "gets it." Both sides are equally important. A client can be served best when his needs are clear and when he can offer wise expressions of those needs. The salesperson is wiser and offers a good service when he leads the client to discover those needs. In the end, they both may be rewarded with a contract, among other things.

As we consider the message of this book, we need to remember that our success is not measured by the terms of a contract. Our success is measured by the rewards that are established in our hearts and minds. We are the ones who set the standards for our life. Whether those standards are based on a moral compass or on our faith, we should honor them and be consistent in our beliefs and in our behavior. In the process we will be personally and professionally rewarded. Our friends, family and associates will take pride and pleasure in knowing us.

Our life counts for many things, but most importantly it counts for how we invest in the lives of people we encounter. Our "net worth" is the sum of our sales abilities and our personal attributes – how we have interacted with others. With eagerness, we can reach out and brighten the world around us. We can live happily while influencing others who follow in our footprints, magnifying our good efforts in being a role model for others. This is one reason why we are here and how we can integrate God's promise in our lifestyles. Please consider joining me on this fascinating and rewarding journey of NetWorthing.

NetWorthing with Polly

"*Always appreciate people
and receive rewards in humility.*"

Worthwhile Reflections

Worth a Million
"The greatest investment we can make is in the life of another person!"

Worth a Thousand Words
"There goes an honorable person; I like doing business with him (or her)."

Worth the Wait
"Anything worth doing is worth doing right!"

Worth Repeating
"Please do it again – do it again!"

Worth the Effort
"You cannot give out enough goodness!"

Worth Sharing
"We should never underestimate the power of the unspoken word!"

Worth Celebrating
"Be blessed as you celebrate the blessings of others!"

Worth Ultimate Praise
"Only God can confirm the hope and joy necessary to live a life of faith."

Worthwhile Conclusion
"Always appreciate people and receive rewards in humility."

About the Author

*P*olly Rhea Harper is truly a Southern lady of personal style and passion who is all about NetWorthing. Her heart becomes entwined around most everyone she meets. It is her mission to connect friends to friends in a variety of ways. She gives God the credit for her special gift.

She is also known in the community for hosting the annual Ladies Brunch in January, celebrating the many friendships she treasures.

Polly has earned significant recognition through her contributions in the Atlanta technology community by investing in the lives of other professionals.

As a key initiator and organizer of the first Atlanta High Tech Prayer Breakfast, founded in 1991, Polly championed the development of the breakfast's leadership team, the Host Committee in the beginning years.

High Tech Ministries, Inc. (HTM), a non-profit Christian organization, still promotes the Annual Breakfast. With attendance as high as sixteen hundred, the breakfast has led to over fifteen different ongoing weekly Bible studies located throughout Atlanta.

Polly is a native of Arkansas and a transplant from Dallas, Texas. She attended Northwestern State in Louisiana, Henderson State and Central Baptist Colleges in Arkansas. She moved to Georgia in 1989 to accept her position with Wm. Leonard & Co. as a licensed real estate agent. She practices relationship marketing as she identifies the office leasing needs of technology companies. Polly resides in Alpharetta, Georgia. Connect with her at www.pollyharper.com.

NetWorthing with Polly

polly@wmleonard.com